BEHIND THE SCENES

HOW A RESTAURANT WORKS

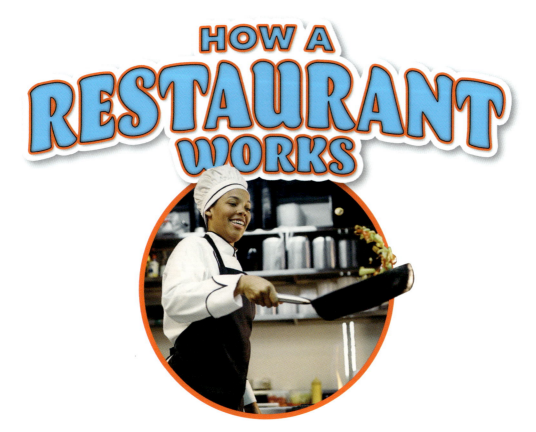

By Jennifer Boothroyd

Consultant: Beth Gambro
Reading Specialist, Yorkville, Illinois

BEARPORT
PUBLISHING

Minneapolis, Minnesota

Teaching Tips

Before Reading

- Look at the cover of the book. Discuss the picture and the title.

- Ask readers to brainstorm a list of what they already know about restaurants. What can they expect to see in the book?

- Go on a picture walk, looking through the pictures to discuss vocabulary and make predictions about the text.

During Reading

- Read for purpose. Encourage readers to think about how a restaurant works as they are reading.

- Ask readers to look for the details of the book. What are some jobs at a restaurant?

- If readers encounter an unknown word, ask them to look at the sounds in the word. Then, ask them to look at the rest of the page. Are there any clues to help them understand?

After Reading

- Encourage readers to pick a buddy and reread the book together.

- Ask readers to name two things that happen at a restaurant. Find the pages that tell about these things.

- Ask readers to write or draw something they learned about restaurants.

Credits

Cover and title page, © Drazen Zigic/iStock; 3, © CareyHope/iStock; 5, © Kobus Louw/iStock; 7, © Ekkasit Jokthong/iStock; 9, © davit85/Adobe Stock; 11, © AnnaStills/iStock; 12–13, andresr/iStock; 15, © FG Trade/iStock; 16–17, annanahabed/Adobe Stock; 19, © FOTOGRAFIA INC./iStock; 20–21, monkeybusinessimages/iStock; 22T, © Francesco Marzovillo/iStock; 22M, © john wreford/Alamy Stock Photo; 22B, © McGhiever/Wikimedia Commons; 23TL, © LeoPatrizi/iStock; 23TM, © AnnaStills/iStock; 23TR, © webphotographeer/iStock; 23BL, © Diamond Dogs/iStock; 23BR, © SolStock/iStock.

See BearportPublishing.com for our statement on Generative AI Usage.

Library of Congress Cataloging-in-Publication Data

Names: Boothroyd, Jennifer, 1972- author.
Title: How a restaurant works / by Jennifer Boothroyd ; consultant Beth
  Gambro, Reading Specialist, Yorkville, Illinois.
Description: Minneapolis, Minnesota : Bearport Publishing Company, [2026] |
  Series: Behind the scenes | Includes bibliographical references and
  index.
Identifiers: LCCN 2024054635 (print) | LCCN 2024054636 (ebook) | ISBN
  9798892329859 (library binding) | ISBN 9798895774168 (paperback) | ISBN
  9798895771020 (ebook)
Subjects: LCSH: Restaurants--Juvenile literature.
Classification: LCC TX945 .B624 2026 (print) | LCC TX945 (ebook) | DDC
  647.95--dc23/eng/20250116
LC record available at https://lccn.loc.gov/2024054635
LC ebook record available at https://lccn.loc.gov/2024054636

Copyright © 2026 Bearport Publishing Company. All rights reserved. No part of this publication may be reproduced in whole or in part, stored in any retrieval system, or transmitted in any form or by any means, electronic, mechanical, photocopying, recording, or otherwise, without written permission from the publisher. Bearport Publishing is a division of FlutterBee Education Group.

For more information, write to Bearport Publishing, 3500 American Blvd W, Suite 150, Bloomington, MN 55431.

Contents

Out to Eat 4

Restaurant Fun Facts 22

Glossary 23

Index 24

Read More 24

Learn More Online 24

About the Author 24

Out to Eat

We are at a restaurant.

A **server** takes our order.

Our meals will be out soon.

How does a restaurant work?

The server has to get our order to the kitchen.

At some restaurants, they use computers.

Sometimes, they write the orders on paper.

The kitchen is very busy.

There are many cooks there.

Each one has a job to do.

This helps the restaurant run smoothly.

Some cooks get **ingredients** ready.

They cut veggies and make **sauces**.

Others put meals together.

> **Say ingredients like in-GREE-dee-ints**

There can be many meals in one order.

The cooks have to work together.

That way, the food will be ready at the same time.

One cook grills meat on a stove.

Another fries food in hot oil.

They put the finished food on plates.

A worker puts the plates on a **warming shelf**.

This keeps food hot until the other meals are ready.

Then, servers bring the order to the table.

After **customers** eat, servers take away the dishes.

Workers wash some dishes in the kitchen sink.

They put others into a dishwasher.

A lot happens at a restaurant.

The food is really tasty.

We like going out to eat!

Restaurant Fun Facts

In the past, some restaurants served only one dish. People did not get to choose their meal.

The world's largest restaurant is in Syria. It can seat more than 6,000 people!

White Castle was the first fast food chain in the United States. It opened in 1921.

Glossary

customers people who come to eat in restaurants

ingredients foods used to make a meal

sauces liquid toppings for food

server a restaurant worker who takes orders and brings out food

warming shelf a shelf that keeps food warm before it is served

Index

dishes 18, 22
ingredients 10
kitchen 6, 8, 18
order 4, 6, 12, 16
server 4, 6, 16, 18
warming shelf 16

Read More

Birdoff, Ariel Factor. *Servers (What Makes a Community?).* Minneapolis: Bearport Publishing Company, 2022.

Rodriguez, Alicia. *Restaurant (I Spy in My Community).* New York: Crabtree Publishing, 2022.

Learn More Online

1. Go to **FactSurfer.com** or scan the QR code below.
2. Enter "**Restaurant Works**" into the search box.
3. Click on the cover of this book to see a list of websites.

About the Author

Jenny Boothroyd worked in restaurants when she was a teenager. She liked working in the dish room. She did not like slicing lots and lots of tomatoes.